Baltimore Album of Roses

Elegant Motifs to Mix & Match
Step-by-Step Techniques—Appliqué, Embroidery, Inking, Trapunto

RITA VERROCA

C&T PUBLISHING

Text copyright © 2015 by Rita Verroca

Photography and artwork copyright © 2015 by C&T Publishing, Inc.

Publisher: Amy Marson

Creative Director: Gailen Runge

Art Director / Cover Designer: Kristy Zacharias

Editor: Lee Jonsson

Technical Editors: Susan Hendrickson and Debbie Rodgers

Book Designer: Christina Jarumay Fox

Production Coordinator: Zinnia Heinzmann

Production Editor: Joanna Burgarino

Illustrator: Aliza Shalit

Photo Assistant: Mary Peyton Peppo

Instructional and quilt photography by Stevie Verroca, unless otherwise noted; additional quilt photography by Diane Pedersen on pages 9, 17, 70, 78, 82, and 89

Published by C&T Publishing, Inc., P.O. Box 1456, Lafayette, CA 94549

Library of Congress Cataloging-in-Publication Data

Verroca, Rita, 1955-

Baltimore album of roses : elegant motifs to mix & match : step-by-step techniques : appliqué, embroidery, inking, trapunto / Rita Verroca.

pages cm

ISBN 978-1-60705-870-0 (soft cover)

1. Patchwork--Patterns. 2. Album quilts--Maryland--Baltimore. I. Title.

TT835.V47 2015

746.46--dc23

2014047450

Printed in China

10 9 8 7 6 5 4 3 2 1

Acknowledgments

Thank you to my loving husband, Steve. I cherish all the support, love and encouragement you have always given me.

Thank you to my wonderful daughters, Stevie and Jessie, who are a great source of pride and constant inspiration. I love you.

A special thanks to my daughter Stevie, who contributed to the book. I am in awe of your work and forever grateful for your patience and exquisite help.

To my friend Sue Messina: thank you for your love, friendship, and generosity.

To all my friends from Rita's Club—Mary Beals, Kathryn Bernstein, Susan Bradshaw, Nadine Cassady, Nancy Chesney-Smith, Barbara Dahl, Mary Fischel, Sue Flynn, Donna Garrity, Ellen Heck, Jessica LaMar, Gladys Lee, Alice Loui, Margaret Russell, Ann Rust, Doreen Smith, Madeline Swope, Edna Tanita, and Roz Thebaud—thank you for your friendship. You keep me in stitches, sew it seams.

Center wreath in *Album of Roses* (page 17)

Dedication

I DEDICATE THIS BOOK TO ALL QUILTMAKERS FROM LONG AGO. THEIR INSPIRING QUILTS ARE SHINING EXAMPLES OF FRIENDSHIP, LOVE, AND PATRIOTISM AND CONVEY TO US A SENSE OF PURPOSE AND BELONGING.

Flowers in
Album of Roses
(page 17)

Contents

Historical View of Baltimore Album Quilts

The history and development of appliqué in America during the 19th century in Baltimore, Maryland, is fascinating and intriguing. Between 1840 and 1852, Baltimore was the second-largest city in America. It was a rich and flourishing city, buzzing with excitement. Trade ships from all over the world made it to American shores, and those vessels brought, among other goods, many fabrics that were exquisite in color, design, and texture. British chintzes, inspired by Indian palampores, depicted flowers in baskets and bouquets, cornucopias filled with fruits, colorful birds, and butterflies of every species. Lively trade brought beautiful cottons, ombrés, and rainbow fabrics from France and England in stunning hues of red, gold, blue, brown, and green, which quilters used to create spectacular examples of appliqué art. Pride, prosperity, happiness, excitement, and the assurance of a better future were reflected in the quilts from this prosperous era, and it is no wonder these quilts inspire us to this day.

BALTIMORE BLOCKS

Since the first Baltimore Album quilts appeared, almost two centuries ago, quilters have been fascinated by these quilts. Often referred to as the "Queen of Quilts," the Baltimore Album quilt has for many decades inspired quilters to recreate these beautiful designs. Trying to replicate the original patterns, fabrics, colors, and textures as closely as possible, today's quilters connect to the past, unveiling and sharing the significance and mystery that surround each block. The early Baltimore Album quiltmakers chose their fabrics with great care and executed the handwork with skillful precision. The blocks they designed and stitched represented their pride, love, ideals, and opinions, leaving us with a vivid account of their place in history. Because we have no written documentation about these blocks, we can only guess what the makers were thinking when they stitched these beautiful appliqué blocks. But it is this mystery that adds interest and romance to these intriguing handmade treasures.

The beautiful blocks we study in this chapter are authentic Baltimore Album blocks, drawn out as patterns by Elly Sienkiewicz in her book *Spoken Without a Word*, unless otheriwse indicated. As noted, many of my students stitched blocks for me, and these blocks are now featured in the *Rita Verroca Friendship Quilt*.

Friendship Quilt designed by Rita Verroca,
border designed and stitched by Rita Verroca

At the beginning of the 19th century, the newly erected George Washington Monument and the Battle Monument, honoring the fallen of the War of 1812, were the pride of Baltimore.

George Washington Monument, 18″ × 18″, pattern drafted and stitched by Rita Verroca

George Washington Monument, 18″ × 18″, stitched by Ann Rust

Battle Monument, 18″ × 18″, pattern drafted and stitched by Rita Verroca

Whose house was the Maryland Manor House? Was it the house of a prominent resident of the city or a city official? Does the eagle that hovers over the house symbolize an important event that occurred in this snapshot of the past? We can only guess.

Maryland Manor House, 18″ × 18″, pattern drafted and stitched by Rita Verroca

The eagle proudly displayed with an open flag showed the love, pride, and devotion women felt for their newly freed country.

Eagle, 18″ × 18″, stitched by Nadine Cassady

Eagle and Harp, 18″ × 18″, stitched by Ellen Heck

This block, featuring a ship in a wreath of flowers, could have been made to honor a sea captain or to celebrate the newly invented steamship. Because Baltimore was a large mariners' city, either could have been the case.

Steamship, 18″ × 18″, stitched by Rita Verroca

Does the Hunting Scene block depict the duck-shooting club at Carroll's Island, a famous club that was still in existence nearly a century later? One might think so, as the block shows water, white fowl, and a retriever—possibly the famous Chesapeake Bay dog, said to be a cross between a spaniel and an otter.

Hunting Scene, 18″ × 18″, stitched by Rita Verroca

Does the Log Cabin block symbolizing the Harrison presidential race show support or disapproval by the maker? The block includes a large pitcher, a huge glass for cider, and even a cider barrel.

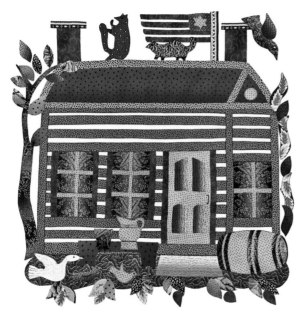

Log Cabin, 18″ × 18″, pattern drafted and stitched by Rita Verroca

Besides the pictorial images depicting events, celebrating news, and recording history, Baltimore Album quilts included a great deal of symbolism, capturing women's ideals and aspirations.

Doves on Bible, 18″ × 18″, stitched by Barbara Dahl

As we search for the makers of these quilts, it is widely assumed that women in churches got together and stitched in groups. The dove, a symbol of the Holy Spirit, is also a symbol of peace and adorns many Baltimore blocks.

Doves on Vase, 18″ × 18″, stitched by Kathryn Bernstein

The pineapple is a symbol of hospitality.

Pineapple, 18″ × 18″, stitched by Madeline Swope

The cornucopia is a symbol of abundance.

Cornucopia, 18″ × 18″, stitched by Mary Beals

Strawberry Wreath, 18″ × 18″, stitched by Susan Bradshaw

Heart of Flowers, 18″ × 18″, stitched by Margaret Russell

Fleur de Lis, 18″ × 18″, stitched by Rosalind Thebaud

Berries and Sprigs, 18″ × 18″, stitched by Nancy Chesney-Smith

Flower Basket, 18″ × 18″, stitched by Jessica LaMar

Flowers bring happiness and make these bright blocks of flowers blaze.

Scherenschnitt, 18″ × 18″, stitched by Rita Verroca

Rose of Sharon, 18″ × 18″, stitched by Mary Fischel

We learn from historical images, absorb and enjoy them. In this book, you will find new blocks that go well with the old patterns and continue the Baltimore tradition.

THE WOMEN WHO STITCHED THEM

Having stitched many Baltimore Album blocks, I feel a certain kinship to the "Ladies of Baltimore." A Baltimore Album quilt dated 1848, currently in the collection of the St. Louis Art Museum, carries the inscription "Presented to E. Morrison By Ladies of Baltimore, Md." We can only guess whether the eight signatures on the quilt positively identify all the makers of this stunning quilt or whether the names stand collectively for a larger group called Ladies of Baltimore. A Baltimore representation quilt was without any doubt a group effort and it is safe to assume that the blocks for this quilt, or any other representation quilt, were specifically chosen and especially designed to honor the recipient. The fact that so many Baltimore Album quilts carry almost identical or at least similar designs leads me to conclude that there was indeed a group of women called the Ladies of Baltimore who were responsible for creating a good number of these exceptional quilts under the patronage and guidance of Achsah Goodwin.

Achsah Goodwin was the daughter of William Goodwin of Lyde. William Goodwin was a wealthy merchant and senior partner in the mercantile house of Goodwin, Russell, and McBride. As William Rush Dunton relates in his book *Old Quilts*, Achsah suffered from a cutaneous disease that left her unable to sew. Despite her medical condition, however, she proceeded to lay out beautiful Broderie Perse quilts, showing her exquisite taste and great talent for design—both of which, according to her daughter, she inherited from her mother. During this time, Maryland was experiencing a great influx of immigrants from Germany and Ireland, who supplied cheap white labor. With the help of slaves or European immigrants, Achsah completed these splendid quilts. It is likely that Achsah's father thought her work was beautiful enough to display in his mercantile house, which would have been a perfect way to showcase new, incoming fabrics and set a trend for the quilters in Baltimore.

Baltimore Album quilts feature a bounty of precious fabrics carefully chosen for their design. Given their quality and cost, these fabrics could not have come from an immigrant's scrap bag. The fact that some of the chintz fabrics Achsah used in her Broderie Perse quilts can be found in some of the Baltimore Album quilts is not a coincidence but provides a direct link between Achsah's Broderie Perse quilts and the Baltimore Album quilts she later designed. I suspect that being the daughter of William Goodwin gave Achsah many opportunities to acquire fine imported chintz and various novelty fabrics, including the brilliant ombrés from France that had come into vogue. Achsah designed a great number of quilts, and quite a few of them are still in excellent condition and can still be viewed at museum quilt exhibits.

When Achsah was eighteen years old she became a Methodist, and a year later she married William Wilkins Jr., another Methodist. William Wilkins Jr. and his father owned a dry goods store on Baltimore Street. Achsah's father, William Goodwin, worshipped at Old St. Paul's Episcopal Church and was, at first, quite dismayed at his daughter becoming a Methodist, but he eventually changed his mind. Achsah became a strong supporter of the Methodist Church and was extremely involved in its activities, which

included fundraising for the church. Described by her daughter as a strong-willed woman with great dignity and charisma, Achsah entertained clergymen and dignitaries from England on a regular basis. Those attributes and the fact that a great number of quilts were connected to the Methodist Church reinforce my belief that Achsah played a vital role in designing the Baltimore Album quilts.

Through her father and her husband, Achsah had access to many fine fabrics, and I suspect she generously contributed not only most of the fabrics but also her time and skill as a talented designer to create these beautiful quilts to raise funds for the church. The diversity of the churchgoing population during this time might explain the multitude of designs we find in the quilts. Interestingly enough, many Europeans brought with them an album, filled with pages of inscriptions from their Old World friends. We find the word "album" written or embroidered on many Baltimore quilts. The word "album" is the same word in English, French, German, Dutch, Irish, and several other European languages.

Amelia Peck wrote in *American Quilts and Coverlets* that Hannah Mary Trimble of Baltimore wrote in her diary on February 1, 1850, that she had visited a Mrs. Simon, and described her as "the lady who cut and basted these handsome quilts." After the discovery of this entry in Hannah Trimble's diary, some scholars believed Mary Simon to be the designer of the Baltimore Album quilts. Mary Simon, born Anna Maria Hergenroder, was a Bavarian immigrant. She was born in 1808, is believed to have arrived in Baltimore in the early 1840s, and married Philip Simon on June 23, 1844—relatively late in her life when you consider the average age of marriage was between 14 and 16 years at that time. Did Mary Simon and other women of European descent design the Baltimore Album quilts, or did they work for Achsah, making kits and samples? Because quilts did not exist in Germany during this time, it would have been very unlikely that Mary Simon would have had the knowledge of American history and the design skill to create these appliqué blocks. But it is likely that she was a fine seamstress, and she could have been hired by the dry goods store on Baltimore Street to "cut and baste" according to Achsah's design. The fact that the Baltimore Album quilt era ended around the same year that Achsah Goodwin died could be further evidence in support of this assumption.

Even with this background, more questions emerge. Did Achsah offer these kits for sale in the family's store? If so, this could explain why we find in various Album quilts so many almost identical blocks, not only in design but also in choice of fabric used. Some quilts from this era show one or two blocks with a very refined design, while other blocks from the same quilt are less sophisticated. Did the makers of these quilts just buy one or two blocks for inspiration because that was all they could afford? One thing is for certain: it is not a coincidence that these blocks are nearly identical; this could only have been possible through the purchase of a kit or pattern. Did Achsah design these blocks, have them cut and basted, and offer them for sale in the store, or did she bring them to weekly church meetings, where they would be sewn together into beautiful quilts? Both scenarios are possible, and the latter idea would not be too far-fetched, as it reminds me of what we as quilters like to do today—meet, stitch, and do some good by sharing the gift of quilting.

Album of Roses

Album of Roses, 101″ × 101″, by Rita Verroca

Flowers in *Album of Roses* center wreath

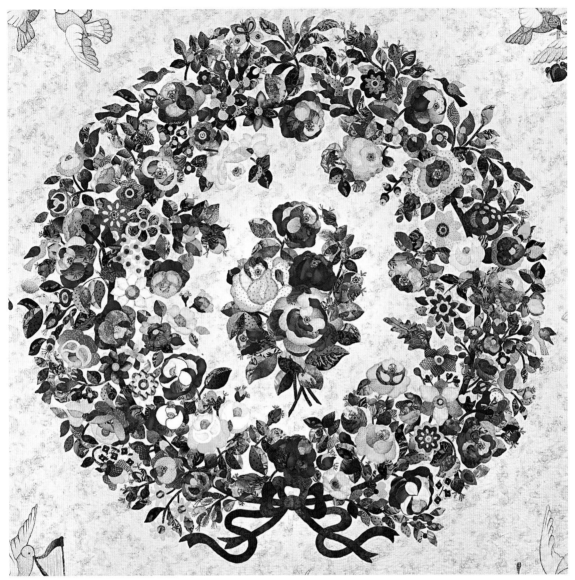

Center wreath in *Album of Roses*

My *Album of Roses* quilt is a celebration of Baltimore Album quilts, made to honor the women who stitched them. The center of the quilt features a bouquet of roses with multilayered petals. These layers give each rose a more realistic appearance and allow the quilter to use various shades of fabrics in one color or a combination of several colors. A wreath of flowers surrounds the rose bouquet and is the focal point of the quilt. Roses of various shapes, colors, and sizes adorn the quilt, celebrating nature and the abundance of its beauty. The roses, rosebuds, and flowers in *Album of Roses* remind us of the flowers in historic Baltimore Album quilts, but the new, layered flowers provide more detail. Hummingbirds and butterflies flit lightly by, while doves, symbolizing love and peace, add grace to this lovely scene. Most Baltimore Album quilts are set in block or album formats, much like the pages of the ladies friendship album books of the time. Each block represents a different, beautiful image. In *Album of Roses*, these traditional elements—baskets of flowers, cornucopias, roses, and flowers—are arranged into swags and garlands, emulating the free-flowing composition of the Broderie Perse bedspreads of the earlier 1800s. In this book, I included an assortment of detail photos from *Album of Roses* to offer readers inspiration and an invitation to find and stitch their own favorite roses or flowers.

Cornucopia in *Album of Roses*

Flowers in *Album of Roses*

Flower basket in *Album of Roses*

How to Achieve a
Baltimore Look

Close-up of flowers in *Album of Roses*

As we travel through American quilt history, it is fascinating to see how closely the quilts were connected to the time when they were made. Women expressed themselves through their quilts, leaving a vivid account of their lives. When cloth was scarce in the early Colonial years, women used whatever fabric was still usable—pieces of clothing not yet worn out, old blankets, and often tiny scraps of homespun fabrics. Because women were not only practical but also eager to beautify their homes, they started to lay out these scraps in beautiful designs and arrange them into blocks. When more fabric became available, women splurged and started to appliqué, sewing one piece of cloth onto another. With beautiful fabrics rolling off American mills, women could now enjoy adding another dimension to their creations. Color, one of the most important elements of a quilt, became more varied. Having more color choices in their fabrics and quilts gave women the opportunity to express their creativity as well as record the sentiment of the nation. During the Baltimore era, this creativity was expressed with a high degree of excellence in workmanship and design. Even today, the quality of the work is unparalleled. Baltimore Album quilts of the 1800s have a very distinct look. Exuberant and glorious in color, quilts of the time featured a multitude of exquisite fabrics, with every piece of fabric carefully chosen to create what we now consider works of art.

COLOR CHOICE

Fabric samples

Many Baltimore Album designs depicted elements of nature. The colors for flowers were carefully chosen, giving each flower its own character. As you set out to create a color palette for your quilt, it is only logical to let nature be your inspiration. Naturally occurring color schemes are both simple and complex. Taking a walk in the garden and looking closely at roses and other flowers will give you infinite possibilities for color arrangements for your quilt. Nature's colors are often highly saturated; bright greens, flaming reds, sunny yellows, and vibrant blues all come to mind. All these colors have strong intensity, or chroma. Just as height, width, and length describe a cube, hue, value, and chroma describe a color. One must analyze a color one dimension at a time to understand its relationship to the others.

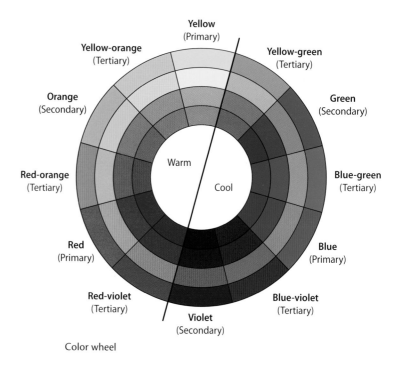

Color wheel

Red, yellow, and blue, which are the primary hues, as well as orange, green, and purple, the secondary hues, all appear in nature and serve as shining examples of color choice possibilities. Hues can be of a lighter tint or darker shade, which creates the value of a color. However, it is the strength or intensity—the chroma—of a color that we want to focus on. Nature's colors are strong. A single wild rose on a hill can be seen from far away, just as a crimson tulip or golden lily in the garden can instantly catch one's eye. As you get ready to pick the colors for your quilt, try to keep these images in mind or have a flower book next to you as you go through your stash. Choose bright fabrics, not muted ones, as nature is vibrant.

Baltimore Album quilts have a bright and happy appearance, and we can sense from them the euphoria America was experiencing during those years. By contrast, quilts made during the Civil War years that followed featured colors that were muted and subdued. Today's beautiful selection of fabrics allows us to create a red rose in multiple hues with petals in lighter tints or darker shades without losing the intensity of the color. A rose or flower with its many petals can take on such a realistic look that the viewer might be tempted to bend down and try to smell its lingering perfume.

Flower basket in *Album of Roses*

FABRIC CHOICE

Baltimore Album quilters used specific fabrics to create dimension, movement, contour, and shading, which gave these beautiful quilts their characteristic look. Choosing similar fabrics today allows us to emulate this beautiful design style.

Ombré fabrics

Look for ombrés (also known as fondu or rainbow fabrics), which are fabrics with graded intensities of the same hue, in solids or sometimes with an overprint. The gradation can be linear, irregular, or random. These shaded fabrics give us the opportunity to pick highs and lows for our design. Cutting from these graded fabrics resembles fussy cutting, but instead of using a particular design from a print in a fabric, you will fussy cut the lighter or darker section of a fabric. As you place your precut template on the fabric, you can determine the particular section you intend to highlight. (Mylar templates work well because they are see-through.)

tip

Suggestions for highlighting:

- Outer edges of leaves and flowers, so they almost look as if the sunshine is brightening them
- Tips of rosebuds
- Tips of paisley-shaped rose petals in a paisley rose
- Any petal of a rose or flower that needs to be brighter
- Flowers with multiple petals, highlighting every other petal
- Bird wings, either the tips of the wings or the wings placed against the body
- Clusters of berries, grapes, or cherries

It is a lot of fun looking for highlights in a fabric, and the search is well worth the effort because well-chosen highlights will add dimension and life to the design.

Highlight on top

Highlight on left side

Highlight on top right side of leaf

Flower highlights in *Album of Roses*

A. Left side of calyx
B. Lighter
C. Lighter
D. Light paisley petal under darker tone
E. Highlighted wing
F. Leaf from light to dark
G. Light tip highlighted
H. Highlight
I. Lighter flower top

Reproduction fabrics with small repeating prints in poison green, Turkey red, blue, brown, yellow, and gold are also well suited to Baltimore-style appliqué because they can add more visual interest to the design than can solid colors.

Fabric samples with small repeating prints

Wavy prints will create the illusion of movement, as if a leaf or flower petal is swaying in the wind.

Example of wavy print

Hand-dyed fabrics come in a multitude of colors and shades and are therefore perfectly suited for roses, flower petals, and leaves. If you prefer a less watercolor look, add a printed petal or a fussy-cut petal or leaf from a bigger print to your design. It will add structure, depth, and realism.

Rose appliqué, made by Ellen Heck

Striped fabrics cut on the diagonal are excellent for vines and stems.
They give the appearance of climbing vines and growing stems and
make flowers and trees look like they are moving in the breeze.

Basket of flowers in *Album of Roses*

Appliqué

READING PATTERNS AND LAYOUTS

The patterns in this book are identified by name. With each project you will find a list of patterns used in making the quilt and a layout diagram that indicates where to position the patterns so they can be traced onto the background fabric. In some projects the patterns are repeated and sometimes used in reverse. To reverse the image, make a photocopy of the pattern, lay the copy upside down on a lightbox, and trace the design. It is now reversed.

The numbers on the patterns indicate the sewing sequence. Begin sewing with the number 1 piece and continue building the design. Some of the designs are marked with letters as well. These letters are subordinate and identify the individual components of the design. They are in alphabetical order and show the sewing sequence for that part of the design. Roses or baskets are often built using this numbering and lettering sequence. You may wish to concentrate on choosing fabrics for a rose, for example, and the letters help focus that task.

The gray lines on the patterns indicate places where you might want to add embroidery (page 48) or button flowers (page 59).

MARKING THE BACKGROUND FABRIC AND CUTTING OUT APPLIQUÉ PIECES

Supplies:

- Master pattern
- Background fabric
- Mylar template plastic
- Pencil with 2B or 3B lead
- Water-soluble marker for light fabrics
- White fabric pencil for dark fabrics
- Double-sided adhesive tape
- Cotton fabrics for appliqué
- Paper scissors
- Fabric scissors

1. Following the layout diagram, trace the design from the master pattern onto the background fabric with a water-soluble marker. (A thick Clover water-soluble marker works well.) The blue lines will help you position the appliqué correctly. However, they do not need to be exactly matched when you sew down the appliqué, as they serve as guidelines only.

2. Trace the design from the master pattern onto the Mylar template plastic and cut out all the shapes for the appliqué. It is very helpful to mark the individual template pieces with their numbers or letters. Sometimes, as with the paisley shapes of a rose, the shapes look similar. Sometimes template pieces flip over, and without a number or letter it is difficult to tell which side is up. A marked template identifies the design and thus ensures the proper position of the appliqué.

3. Place the Mylar pieces on the bias of the fabric. This is important. The bias of a woven fabric lies at 45° to its warp and weft threads. Woven fabric is more elastic and fluid in the bias direction. By positioning the shapes on the bias, you will utilize the greater stretch of the fabric, and as a result the pieces will be easier to appliqué. Use tightly woven fabrics—fabrics with a higher thread count—as they produce a smooth, crisp edge more easily than do fabrics with a low thread count.

4. Use a white fabric pencil to mark shapes on dark fabric and a water-soluble marker for lighter fabric. Cut out all the shapes, leaving a ¾6″ seam allowance.

Pattern traced onto fabric with water-soluble marker

tip

Lay out your appliqué design on paper. I enlarge the paper pattern by 10% using a copier. This will ensure room for the seam allowance. After I cut the shapes out of fabric, I fasten them with double-sided adhesive tape onto the paper enlargement. This way I can check my color choices before the pieces are sewn down and easily replace one or two pieces if the design I laid out does not appeal to me.

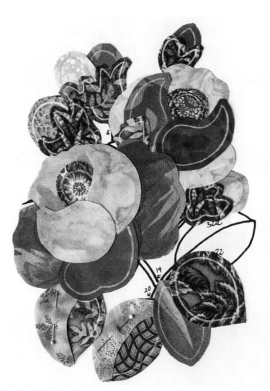

Appliqué design layout on paper

Appliqué design layout on paper

Partial appliqué with flower layout on paper

Appliqué design layout on paper

Butterfly layout

Finished butterfly

Sometimes I just cut out a flower, stick the fabric pieces onto the paper, and lay it on my appliqué that is already sewn to check whether the colors work together. Also, if you've already designed your flower on paper, you can relax and concentrate on your sewing.

PINNING

Supplies:

- Silk pins or Clover patchwork pins

As the words "needle turn" imply, you will use your sewing needle or silk pins as a tool to turn under the seam allowance. Clover patchwork pins are wonderful to use for pinning, as they go through the fabric smoothly. I will demonstrate the technique by preparing and pinning a stem.

1. Place the fabric in front of you at a 45° angle. All the appliqué pieces will be cut on the bias unless you fussy cut a design in the fabric. Draw a line the length of the stem. This will be your cutting line.

2. Draw another line parallel to this line, ³⁄₁₆" to the right. This will be your sewing line. Draw a third parallel line to the right, with the distance determined by how wide you want the stem, and yet another line ³⁄₁₆" beyond that line for the other cutting line. In the end you will have a piece that is the width of the stem plus a ³⁄₁₆" seam allowance on either side.

3. Cut out the stem and place it on the background fabric. I work on a flat surface while pinning to make sure the image lies flat. Hold the stem in position by placing silk pins ½" parallel to and just to one side of the center line, about 1" apart. This is necessary because fabric on fabric "travels," and you want to make sure that the appliqué piece stays in place while you turn under the seam allowance.

Pin parallel to center line to hold fabric.

Because the stem is cut on the bias, you need to be sure not to stretch the fabric, especially if the stem is bent. On curved lines and bias-cut stems, pin the inner curves first to avoid puckers.

4. Pinch the seam allowance and turn it under where you will start sewing, and pin the edge that has been turned under to the background fabric. Moving 1" to the left, pinch the seam allowance again, turn it under, and pin to the background fabric.

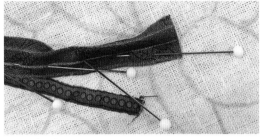

Pin appliqué.

5. Using the side of the needle, swipe under the seam allowance from left to right in a direction I call "9 to 5," starting in the 9 o'clock position, swiping around, and ending in the 5 o'clock position. While swiping from left to right, let your left hand walk over the turned-under seam allowance. Pin about every ¼" slightly to the left, catching the folded edge. You can now remove the horizontally placed pins. If you want to pin another section, do the same. Pin about 1" ahead, swipe, and pin.

9 to 5; turning the seam allowance under

You are now ready to appliqué.

Swag, detail of *Album of Roses*

NEEDLE-TURN TECHNIQUE

Supplies:

- Hand-sewing needles—size 10 or 11 sharps
- 100% cotton thread that matches your appliqué fabric—Aurifil, DMC, or Mettler 60

Appliqué requires hand-eye coordination involving both hands. The left hand does as much work as the right hand if you are right-handed, and vice versa if you are left-handed. For right-handed appliquéing, the left hand holds down the turned-under edge while you apply the blind stitch. You can feel with your left thumb whether the seam allowance is lying flat or whether you have creases (also called noses) in the seam allowance that you need to smooth out. Your left hand, usually your middle finger, will feel the needle on the underside of the background fabric and guide it back to the top. As the left hand steadies the appliqué, the right hand will do the sewing. Be patient while your hands get used to their chores. Everything worthwhile takes a while to learn, but it is well worth the effort because all you'll need for your future appliqué are needles, pins, and thread.

The basic appliqué stitch is a blind stitch. I use a size 11 sharps needle and 100% cotton thread (Aurifil, DMC, or Mettler 60). If needle-turn appliqué is new to you, you might want to use a size 10 sharps needle, as it is a little firmer.

1. Choose a thread that matches the appliqué fabric. Knot the end, bring your needle up from the wrong side of the background fabric just below the folded edge, and slip the needle in and out again through the turned-under seam allowance.

2. Reinsert the needle into the background fabric, repeating the blind stitch.

 tips

Here are a few tips to make sure your appliqué stitches are "blind":

- Your thread will be in your appliqué piece. Insert your needle slightly under the appliqué piece into the background fabric so that the thread winds around the appliqué at an angle. While you do this, move the appliqué slightly upward to make sure you insert the needle under the appliqué into the background fabric. This way your stitch will "sink" into the appliqué.

- Take tiny "bites" from your appliqué piece. Pull the thread tight but not too tight, as the thread never gets tighter but can loosen a bit over time. The smaller the appliqué image, the closer the stitches. I count about 10–12 stitches per inch on my appliqué. As you move ahead on your appliqué, don't forget to pin. You should feel a pin under your left thumb at all times while you appliqué. This will ensure a smooth and flat stitch. If your stitch is visible, the stitch into the background fabric is placed too high or you are taking too big a bite out of the appliqué fabric.

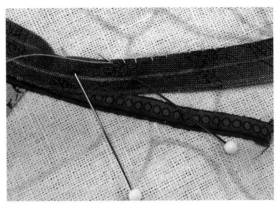

Wrong appliqué stitch

- When you appliqué a multilayered image, you only need to appliqué the exposed seams. Slip a running stitch through the raw edges where the pattern pieces overlap. When you appliqué an image that is fully enclosed, clip away the background fabric, leaving a ¼" seam allowance, before you appliqué the next layer.

Cut away background fabric (back of piece shown on left, front of piece on right).

SKINNY STEMS

The normal seam allowance for any needle-turn appliqué is ³⁄₁₆". To sew a stem that is smaller in width than the regular seam allowance of ³⁄₁₆", mark and cut a stem as described in Pinning (page 35). Proceed to needle-turn a side of the stem.

Sew side of stem.

1. Before you sew the other side, open up the stem and cut away the seam allowance to less than ⅛" all along the sewn seam.

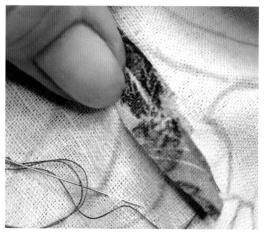

Cut sewn-under seam allowance.

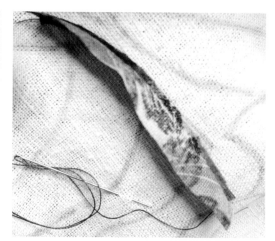

Cut all the way.

2. Turn the appliqué back and cut some of the original ³⁄₁₆" seam allowance. Disregard the original marked line.

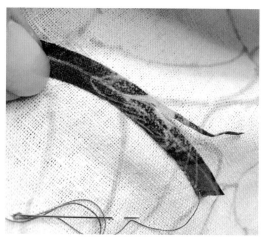

Cut seam allowance on other side.

3. Pin the turned-under seam allowance and appliqué.

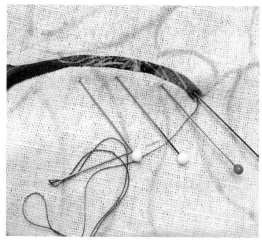

Pin and appliqué.

POINTY LEAVES

1. Mark and cut the leaf, leaving a ³⁄₁₆″ seam allowance.

2. Stitch to the point of the leaf, with your last stitch positioned on the marked line. Double up on this stitch, as it locks the appliqué in place.

3. With your needle or pin, prick into the seam allowance and, carrying the fabric on your needle, move the needle counterclockwise toward the seam you just sewed.

Place stitch into point of leaf.

Pointy point, needle-turned tip of leaf

4. Hold it in place with your thumb and glide your needle in between the layers until it feels nice and smooth. The seam allowance should lie nicely folded under your thumb. If it feels bumpy, you probably "stuffed" the seam allowance. Turn the seam allowance back out and retry. Take a stitch into the tip of the leaf. Take another stitch into the background fabric, placing your needle a little higher than before, and emerge on the upper left side of the leaf.

5. Place a pin ½″ ahead, swipe under the seam allowance, and continue with the appliqué.

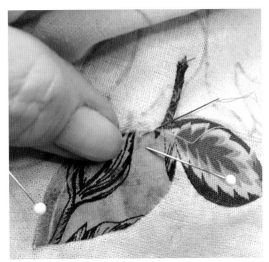

Pin ahead and continue with appliqué.

INVERTED VALLEYS

When you needle-turn curved lines, you need to clip the seam allowance. Outward curving lines, or convex lines, do not need to be clipped. Inward curving lines, or concave lines, do need to be clipped.

1. Clip the seam allowance up to the marked sewing line but not beyond it. If your indentation is deep, cut a "bird's foot" into the seam allowance.

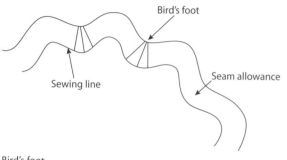

Bird's foot

2. Clip into the deepest part of the indentation. Cut at an angle slightly to the left, then to the right, as shown in the diagram. Your cuts will remind you of a bird's foot. If the indentation has a shallow curve, make small parallel cuts into the seam allowance.

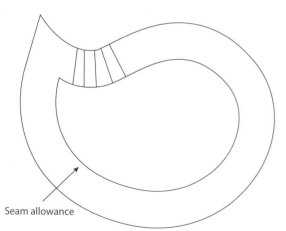

Shallow curve, parallel cuts

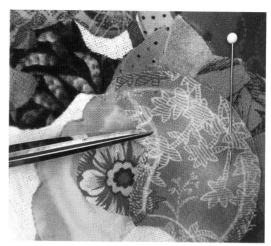

Cut seam allowance of shallow curve.

3. Appliqué to the beginning of the "valley." Fasten the appliqué to the background fabric by positioning a pin ½" under the indentation. This is done to ensure that the appliqué fabric does not "travel" on the background fabric while you turn under the seam allowance. Pinch the seam allowance on the left of the indentation, turn under, and pin. This way your appliqué has little "wiggle room."

Pin inverted valley.

4. Holding your pin or needle at an angle, swipe the seam allowance under in a 9-to-5 motion.

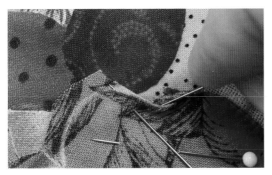

9-to-5 motion, concave

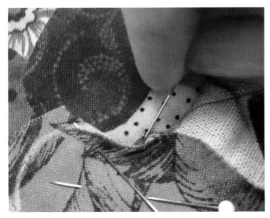

9-to-5 motion

9-to-5 motion, continued

5. Pin and sew.

INVERTED V'S

1. To prepare an inverted V, or sharp inside point, on the appliqué, clip into the V up to the marked line but not beyond it.

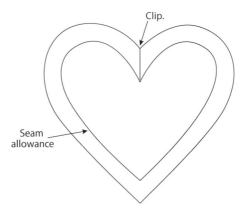

Inverted V

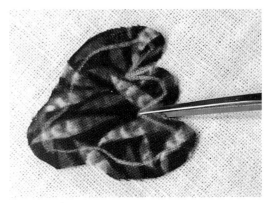

Cut inverted V.

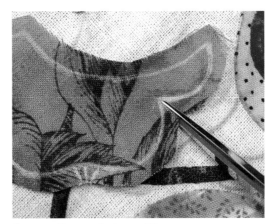

Cut seam allowance for inverted V.

2. Pin the appliqué shape to the background fabric, positioning a pin horizontally ½" under the indentation. Start to needle turn.

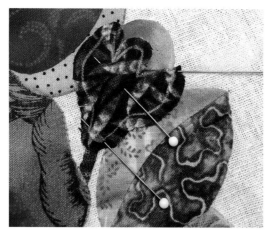

Pin left side of V.

3. As you approach the inverted V, about ½" from the incision, place a pin on the left side of the V to reduce the "wiggle room." Slide your needle into the V and, pulling the needle toward you, swipe under the seam allowance in a 9-to-5 motion.

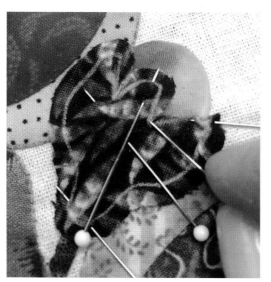

Position of needle in V

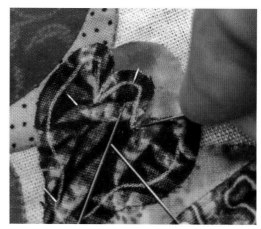

9-to-5 motion in V

4. In the V, take a deeper stitch than for a regular appliqué stitch, about ¹⁄₁₆" in length, right under the incision, catch-ing the background fabric. Repeat the deeper stitch, catching the appliqué fabric only. Take another stitch, now catching the background fabric as well.

Deep stitch in V

5. Turn under the fabric on the left side of the V and proceed to appliqué.

Close-up flowers

SPLIT LEAVES

Split leaves add depth, dimension, and liveliness to appliqué. Rather than splitting a leaf by a straight line as we see done in many Baltimore Album quilts, I prefer sewing a curved split, emulating nature's beauty. In contrast to all other appliqué, I sew the split leaves "off-block," which means that I sew the spilt of the leaf before I appliqué the leaf to the background fabric.

1. Cut out the template and mark the full leaf onto the background fabric.

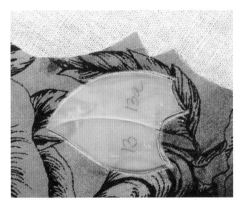

Mark template on background fabric.

2. Cut the template on the curved marked line and draw the line onto the marked leaf on the fabric.

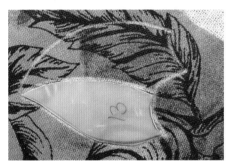

Cut template and mark line on marked full leaf.

3. Take the moon-shaped part of the leaf, mark it on a different fabric, and cut it out, leaving a ³⁄₁₆" seam allowance.

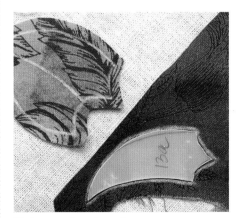

Mark moon-shaped template.

4. Prepare the moon-shaped wedge for appliqué by clipping small parallel incisions into the seam allowance.

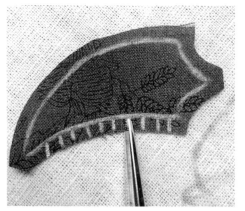

Cut shallow inverted curve.

5. Pin and sew the "moon" section to the full leaf along the marked sewing line. Stitch to the point, but no further, and secure with a second stitch.

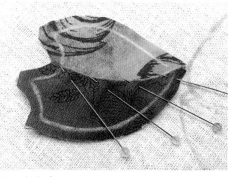

Pin split leaf.

Sew split leaf.

6. Cut away the extra fabric from the underside of the leaf, leaving a ³⁄₁₆" seam allowance.

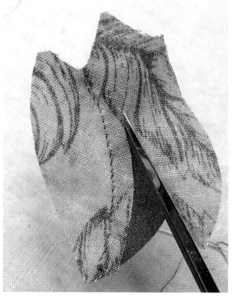

Cut excess fabric.

7. Line up the leaf with the pattern, pin, and start to appliqué.

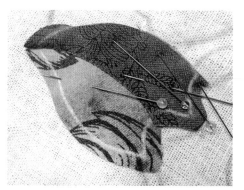

Pin and appliqué.

8. As you approach the tip of the leaf, separate the seam allowance at the point and pin the left side of the leaf to the left and the right side of the leaf to the right. Turn under the seam allowance on the right side of the leaf to the right and sew down.

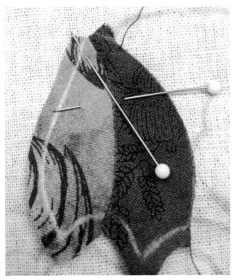

Turn under seam allowance to right.

9. If the left side of the leaf is much lighter than the right side, you will need to change the color of your thread. Travel with the darker thread to the back of the appliqué and take a few backstitches to secure the thread. Rethread your needle with a lighter color of thread. Turn the seam allowance on the left side of the leaf to the left, connecting the 2 sections with a single stitch.

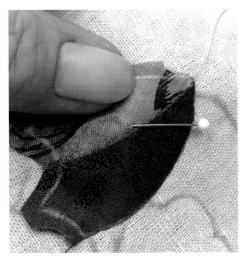

Turn left side of leaf to left.

REVERSE APPLIQUÉ

Reverse appliqué is the technique in which the piece of material that lies under the appliqué is exposed. This could be the background or another piece of material. The viewer gets to discover what is under the first layer of appliqué, and the technique adds dimension and depth to the design. The following example shows reverse appliqué on a rosebud.

1. Cut the template for the rosebud. Then cut out the section that will be reverse appliquéd. Mark the rosebud template onto the fabric, including the section that is to be reverse appliquéd, and cut it out, leaving a ³⁄₁₆″ seam allowance.

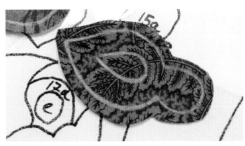

Mark rosebud on fabric.

2. Using the same template, mark only the top section of the contrasting fabric (shown here in red).

Mark fabric for reverse appliqué.

3. Cut the fabric for the reverse appliqué on the inside of the marked line.

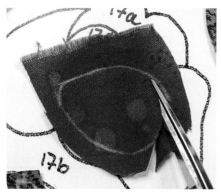

Cut fabric for reverse appliqué.

4. Using a small running stitch, sew the red fabric close to the edge onto the back of the rosebud (the right side of the red fabric to the wrong side of the green fabric).

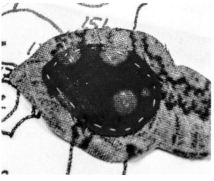

Small running stitch

This shows the rosebud with the running stitch on the right side of the fabric.

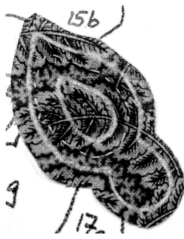

Rosebud with running stitch

5. Appliqué in place.

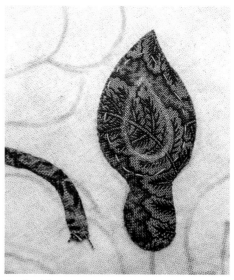

Appliquéd rose

6. Cut the marked design for the reverse appliqué from top to bottom. Make sure you cut only the top layer of fabric. Cut small incisions all around.

Cut seam allowance.

7. Turn under the seam allowance, pin, and sew.

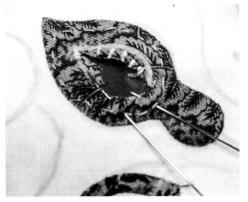

Pin and sew.

8. Remove the basting stitch.

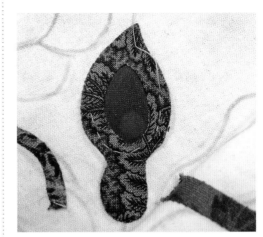

Remove basting.

Flowers from *Album of Roses*

Embroidery

Using embroidery on a quilt is a matter of taste. If you like the look and enjoy enhancing your quilt with embroidery, I would encourage you to do so. After all, it is yourself you express in a quilt, and embroidery will demonstrate your keen eye and show off your love for detail.

Embroidery can outline a contour, highlight, and add detail to an appliqué. The embroidery stitches I used in *Album of Roses* and in the projects in this book are very basic stitches.

Outline stitch for contour: The rose in the ruby slipper consists of white petals. To visually separate the overlapping pattern pieces, outline the petals with a single-stranded outline stitch in red. This gives the rose definition, dimension, and contour. Embroider an outline stitch along the top or side of a rose petal to enhance the shape against the background fabric.

Detail of *Ruby Slipper*

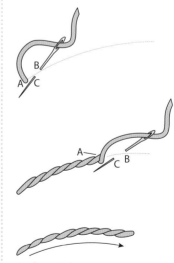

Outline stitch

French knots in *Album of Roses*

Detail of corner unit from *Ruby Slipper*

French knot: If a flower is small but needs a bit of color in the center, embroider a cluster of French knots in the center and see the flower come alive.

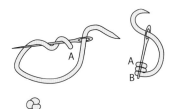

French knot

Decorative straight stitches: Another lovely eye-catcher is an embroidered rose center. To make it colorful, use single strands of different colors of embroidery floss and vary the stitch length: small stitches in green followed by longer stitches in yellow and gold. Embroider single French knots in yellow, pink, and red.

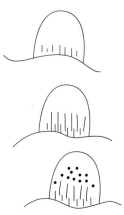

Stitch diagram for rose center

Sometimes an appliquéd stem might seem too heavy for a small leaf. To give the stem an elegant look and a feel of lightness, embroider the stem with a stem stitch. Use a single thread and embroider a second stem in a lighter color parallel to the first if you would like the stem to appear thicker.

Raised stem stitch: Another beautiful embroidery stitch is the raised stem stitch. It is worked from a base of straight stitches upon which rows of stem stitches sit. I used a single strand of variegated embroidery floss to create the design on the shoe in *Ruby Slipper*. Appliqué the shoe and mark the embroidery design on the fabric with a marking pen.

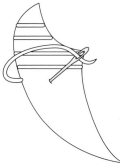

Marking embroidery design

Fill out the marked design with evenly spaced stitches about ⅛″ apart.

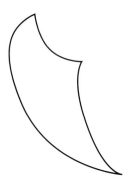

Evenly spaced stitches

Using a new thread, bring up the needle at the very left of the design and pull up.

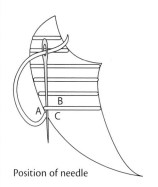

Position of needle

Move the needle from right to left under the first straight stitch and pull gently downward. The needle will loop around the straight stitch rather than going through the fabric.

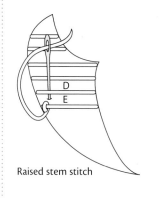

Raised stem stitch

Pull the needle from right to left under the next straight stitch and continue in the same way until you get to the end of the design. Travel underneath to the starting point and sew another row of loop stitches. Repeat until the design is finished.

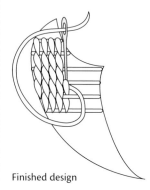

Finished design

Detail of *Ruby Slipper*

Inking

Roses in white, yellow, peach, and pink with multiple petals of the same hue in lighter tones are well worth stitching. They give the needle artist the opportunity to play with one color and its tints and shades and to design a rose or flower that truly resembles the real thing. To enhance the shape of the individual petals, outline the contour with inking. During the Baltimore Album era, quilters used black ink and drew the shape of the petal onto the appliquéd petal to emphasize its shape.

Historical Baltimore block, Lincoln, Nebraska

Black inking on white rose

Today's tools allow us to take a more sophisticated approach to inking. In the more recent past, quilters used oil pastels to shade or highlight an image. But this technique rubs off over time and cannot withstand a good wash. Because I like to use my quilts as bedcovers to sleep under or cuddle with, I never forget that I need to be able to wash my quilts. Shading your quilt with a Pigma pen will give you the desired effect of contouring, and it's easy to do and will stay on permanently.

Tools for inking

1. For lighter roses and flowers, take a brown Pigma pen (size 005) and gently rub the side of the pen tip against the sewn-under edge of the appliqué. Follow up with small gentle lines or strokes at the top edge of the appliqué.

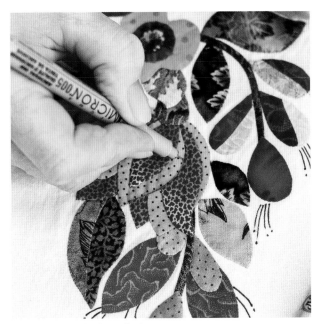

Marking appliqué edge with Pigma pen

2. As soon as you have drawn or applied a 1" line onto the appliqué edge, drag an eraser marker (the Clover eraser marker works well) over the lines you just drew. This will disperse the ink into the fabric and give a shadowed effect.

Marking with eraser pen

3. Continue working along the appliquéd edge, applying a little ink at a time and painting over it with the water-soluble marker. This will give your image a soft, painted edge.

Appliqué detail with no inking

Appliqué detail with inking

A brown Pigma pen will give a white rose a brownish edge, a yellow rose or tulip a golden edge, and a pink or peach rose a matching but darker edge. Practice on a small piece of fabric using a Pigma pen (size 005) until you feel confident and get a feel for the pen. Later you can use a size 01 Pigma pen for a thicker line. You'll be surprised how a little ink can turn a seemingly flat rose into a distinct work of art. Set the color by ironing over the inked surface. The doves on my *Album of Roses* quilt are shown as nature beautifully created them in shades of white, gray, and beige. Here too, I used the inking technique to add detail to the image. With the help of a sepia or black Pigma pen (size 01), I drew in the feathers of the wings and tails by outlining the contours of the birds in this manner. This way, the white doves and little birds clearly stand out from the background fabric as if they were floating in a fragrant air.

Doves with heart in *Album of Roses*

Pink bird in *Album of Roses*

Doves with letter in *Album of Roses*

Blue bird in *Album of Roses*

Quilting

I am a passionate hand quilter and would like to tell you in a few words why I hand quilt. The first time I saw a quilt, it was pictured in an antiques magazine. What immediately caught my eye and fascinated me most was the texture of the background fabric. I had never seen texture like this before, and I set out to find this "bubbly" fabric, as I called it. You see, I thought this was a textured material one could purchase by the yard. Little did I know! As I combed through the fabric stores in Los Angeles in search of my bubbly fabric, the sales clerks kept shaking their heads and telling me that they did not carry this kind of material, and the machine-quilted fabrics from the baby section of the store were not at all what I was looking for. I was looking for that beautiful fabric with thousands of little dimples in it.

When I was almost at my wit's end, an elderly lady explained to me that this kind of thing was created by hand: with a top layer, a filler, and a backing, all held together by a running stitch. She went on to say that the motif made by the tiny stitches in my picture was a clamshell design and that this design was drawn onto the top layer before the three layers were put together. Well, I had something to go by, I thought, and off I went. But no matter how hard I tried, my stitches did not look anything like the stitches in the picture, and, needless to say, I had no dimples either. Then one day when I was sitting in the park stitching and watching my daughter play on the swings, a lady came over and asked me whether I was a quilter. I had never heard that word and asked her to please repeat her question. "A quilter," she said. "Aren't you quilting?" I looked at my hands, still puzzled about what she was talking about. She asked me if I knew the quilt store in town, not

far from where we were. I thanked her and said my good-bye in a hurry. What I was doing had a name, and there were stores for this kind of thing.

As I approached the store I could not believe my eyes. There, right in front of me, was my bubbly fabric with tiny little stitches and thousands of dimples in a beautiful Star of Bethlehem quilt. A lovely lady in the shop, Dolores Wolff, showed me right there how to quilt. I was amazed at the size of her needle. So tiny. I had been stitching with a thick, long needle, since I was going through all those layers of fabric. I was in awe of how she moved the needle up and down through the fabric (not like sewing at all), and how three fingers could fit onto the tiny needle. There and then I fell in love with what I then found out was quilting. I have been quilting ever since, and over time my stitches have gotten smaller.

When you hand quilt a quilt, your stitches make tiny dimples and create the effect of light and dark. This gives a hand-quilted quilt that soft, almost hazy, inviting, very unique look. When you hand quilt a quilt, you create a very special texture, feel, and appearance that cannot be compared with any other material. Hand quilting does not disturb the integrity of the cloth. When you "weave" your quilting thread through the fabrics, you weave the layers of fabric together, making it one unit. The layers don't get squished together but rather woven together. A hand-quilted quilt is never stiff but has a beautiful drape. No matter how close the quilting lines are to each other, the quilt stays wonderfully soft; when I hand quilt my quilts, I ensure myself a cozy cuddle for years to come.

Trapunto

In *Flower Basket with Swags* I added trapunto—also known as *tra punto*, the Italian word for quilting—to my hand quilting. Gracefully raised above other quilting, the trapunto section adds dimension, as it increases the effect of light and shadow. In former days, trapunto was worked by having additional padding forced through the backing of the quilt after the quilt had been quilted. To accomplish this, the quiltmaker would choose a coarser weave for the background fabric, gently pull the threads of the backing fabric apart, stuff a particular chosen section with batting or cotton, and rearrange the treads by pulling them back into their former place. To make things a bit easier, follow these simple steps to sew a trapunto feather.

1. Lay the feather design from the book under the quilt top and trace the design onto the quilt top with a water-soluble marker.

Draw feather design onto quilt top.

Drawn feather design

2. Pin a piece of thin sheer cotton onto the back of the design.

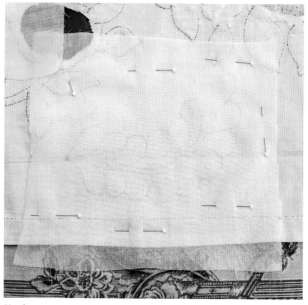

Pin sheer cotton.

3. With a water-soluble thread, sew a small running stitch along the marked lines. Do not cross over the empty spaces, as this will hinder your stuffing later. Backtrack on the previously sewn line.

Sew along lines with water-soluble thread.

4. Cut small incisions into each feather pocket of the sheer fabric.

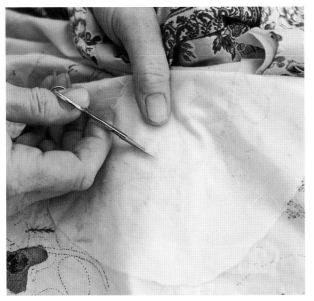

Cut sheer fabric.

5. Take small amounts of leftover batting (I prefer cotton batting, as it will prevent pilling) and, with the help of a toothpick, stuff the pockets evenly. Don't overstuff, as that will make the feather too firm and your quilting later too tight.

Rip small pieces of batting.

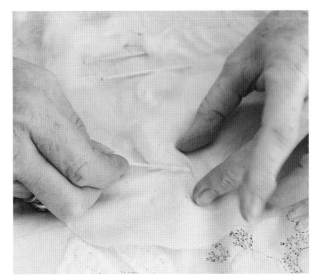

Stuff with toothpick.

tip

For small skinny shapes like stems of flowers, vines, or in this case the shaft of the trapunto feather, proceed as follows:

■ Thread a tapestry needle with a soft multi-ply cotton yarn and double it over so the tail ends meet.

■ Gently separate the threads at the beginning of the shaft and wiggle the tip of the needle under the sheer fabric, pulling it gently to the end of the shaft. Using a rubber finger tip is very helpful for this.

■ After you exit the shape, clip both ends, leaving ⅛″ of the yarn on each end. Tuck and the ends will disappear into the shape.

6. Close the pockets with small stitches using regular sewing thread. Cut the sheer fabric all around, leaving a ½" margin around the image.

Finished trapunto from back side

7. When you are ready to quilt, quilt over the water-soluble thread with quilting thread. (*Hint:* Trapunto looks especially beautiful when you quilt a grid around it.) You have now added trapunto to your quilt.

Button Flowers

Button flowers are cute little fillers. Place them in areas that need a hint of color or sprinkle them into your appliqué wherever there is a bit of open space. You can make a few at a time and have them handy when you work on your appliqué. I used them in *Ruby Slipper* and in the *Little Flower Basket* project.

1. Cut several circles from 1″ to 1¼″ in diameter.

Circles of fabric

2. Gather all around with a small running stitch and pull tight.

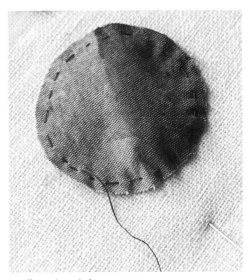

Small running stitch

Pull tight.

3. Using the same thread, secure the gathered circle by stitching up and down through the middle a few times. Do not cut the thread.

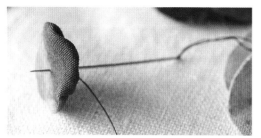

Fasten thread.

4. With a marking pen, mark dots evenly all around the circle. For a 1¼" gathered circle, I marked 5 dots for 5 petals.

Marking circle

5. With the same needle and thread, travel through the layers to the first marked dot and emerge.

Direction of needle

6. Travel back to the middle, taking small stitches through all the layers.

Small stitches

7. Pull tight and secure the gather by going up and down the middle a few times. Repeat, traveling to the next marked dot. Go all around and fasten the thread on the back of the flower. Clip the thread.

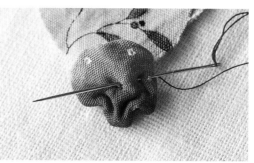

Pull tight.

8. Highlight the middle of your little button flower with a French knot and sew it onto your appliqué project.

French knot

Little Album of Roses

Finished quilt: 62½″ × 62½″

Designed with components from *Album of Roses* (page 17), this project will bring a little Baltimore beauty into your life. The cornucopias and swags from *Album of Roses* make up the frame surrounding the basket from *Flower Basket with Swags* (page 70). The rose that sits in the swag is repeated four times. This chapter includes three other rose designs for you to choose from. Repeat the same flower or stitch a different flower for each of the swags. I hope the multitude of photos in this book will inspire you to create your own *Little Album*.

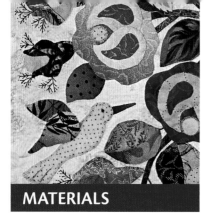

General Instructions: The cutting instructions for background fabrics include a ¼" seam allowance, which adds up to an additional ½" for the length and width measurements. Add your favorite seam allowance when you use the templates for the appliqué.

MATERIALS

- **Background:** 4 yards white, off-white, or light-colored fabric (A white print on white is harder to appliqué onto.)
- **Batting:** 70" × 70"
- **Backing:** 4 yards
- **Binding:** ⅞ yard

- **Fabrics for appliqué:** Choose a variety of tightly woven fabric scraps, from thumb size to fat quarters. If you appliqué a lot as I do, you will find a spot for the last scrap of your favorite fabric, as small as it might be. Maybe the rosebud you will use it for will become your favorite flower in the quilt. For guidance on color and fabric selection, see How to Achieve a Baltimore Look (page 23).

CUTTING

White, Off-White, or Light Color

Background pieces are cut a little larger to allow for tightening during appliqué.

- Cut 4 squares 20" × 20".
- Cut 4 rectangles 20" × 28".
- Cut 1 square 28" × 28".

Binding

- Cut binding fabric on the bias into 2" strips and piece to total 266" (approximately 7½ yards).

CONSTRUCTION

Find and Trace Patterns

- Large Basket*—pattern pullout page P4 (enlarge 125%)
- Garland Part 1—pattern pullout page P2
- Garland Part 2—pattern pullout page P3
- Cornucopia—pattern pullout page P2
- Rose 1—page 65
- Rose 2—page 66
- Rose 3—page 67
- Rose 4—page 68

* Optional: Replace Large Basket with Center Rose—pattern pullout page P3 and enlarge 125%.

Note: The gray lines on the patterns indicate places where you might want to add embroidery (page 48) or button flowers (page 59).

From your master pattern, trace the pattern of the large basket, the bird, and the butterflies onto the 28" × 28" square with a water-soluble marker. Continue by marking the cornucopias onto the 20" × 20" squares. Mark the swags onto the 20" × 28" rectangles and the rose or roses of your choice in the middle of the swags. I mark each pattern one at a time, not all at once, as the water-soluble marker might fade over time.

Appliqué

The numbers on the master pattern indicate the sewing sequence. Follow the sewing sequence and appliqué. For in-depth coverage of this subject, see Appliqué (pages 32–47), which will give you step-by-step instructions and helpful advice to complete your appliqué project.

QUILT ASSEMBLY

Trim the center square to 26½″ × 26½″.

Trim the corner squares to 18½″ × 18½″.

Trim the side rectangles to 18½″ × 26½″.

Follow the quilt layout diagram to sew the blocks together to form the quilt.

FINISHING

Layer, quilt as desired, and finish by binding the quilt.

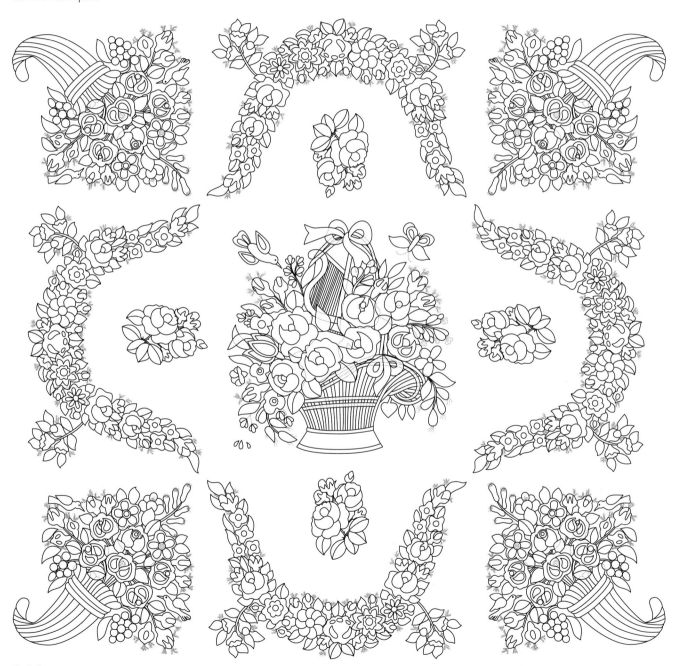

Quilt layout

Cornucopia

Rose 1

Pattern for Rose 1

Rose 2

Pattern for Rose 2

Pattern for Rose 3

Rose 3

Rose 4

4

6

5

7a

8a

7

8

1a

1

3

2

14

9

17

21a

22

10

18

21

16

20

25

25a

15

20a

27

19

11

26

23

24

24a

23a

25

Pattern for Rose 4

13

12

Layout variation, *Little Album of Roses* with center rose motif

Flower Basket with Swags

Finished quilt: 50½″ × 50½″

The flower basket in this quilt, one of the baskets from my *Album of Roses* quilt, is a touch of Baltimore appliqué that will capture your imagination. Framed by graceful swags and embellished with single roses, this quilt will bring you many happy hours of stitching. It will give you the opportunity to create beautiful flowers using bits and pieces of fabrics in the Baltimore style and continue the art for future generations to enjoy.

General Instructions: The cutting instructions for background fabrics include a ¼" seam allowance, which adds up to an additional ½" for the length and width measurements. Add your favorite seam allowance when you use the templates for the appliqué.

MATERIALS

- **Background:** 1¼ yards white, off-white, or light-colored fabric (A white print on white is harder to appliqué onto.)
- **Fabrics for appliqué:** Choose a variety of tightly woven fabric scraps, from thumb size to fat quarters. If you appliqué a lot as I do, you will find a spot for the last scrap of your favorite fabric, as small as it might be. Maybe the rosebud you will use it for will become your favorite flower in the quilt. For guidance on color and fabric selection, see How to Achieve a Baltimore Look (page 23).

- **Fabric for trapunto:** ½ yard sheer white cotton
- **Inner border:** ¼ yard red fabric
- **Outer border:** 1½ yards (For this quilt, I used a pillar print fabric.)
- **Batting:** 58" × 58"
- **Backing:** 3¼ yards
- **Binding:** ¾ yard

CUTTING

White, Off-White, or Light Color
Background pieces are cut a little larger to allow for tightening during appliqué.
- Cut 1 square 38" × 38".

Inner Border (Red)
- Cut 4 strips 1" × 37½".

Outer Border
- Cut 4 strips 7" × 50½". These measurements might differ depending on the width of the border print you choose. Adjust the measurements as you see fit.

Binding
- Cut binding fabric on the bias into 2" strips and piece to total 218" (approximately 6 yards).

CONSTRUCTION
Find and Trace Patterns

- Large Basket—pattern pullout page P4
- Swags 1, 2, 3, and 4—pattern pullout page P1
- Small Rose 1—page 74
- Small Rose 2—page 74
- Small Rose 3—page 75
- Small Rose 4—page 75
- Bow 1—page 76
- Bow 2—page 76
- Trapunto Feather 1—page 72
- Trapunto Feather 2—page 72

Note: The gray lines on the patterns indicate places where you might want to add embroidery (page 48) or button flowers (page 59).

For correct placement, find the center of your background fabric and line it up with the center of the Large Basket master pattern. (As a guide, you can draw an 18" square for the center basket inside the 36" marked block.) Trace the pattern onto the fabric with a water-soluble marker.

Follow the quilt layout diagram (page 73) for correct placement of swags, roses, and bows. I mark each pattern one at a time, not all at once, as the water-soluble marker might fade over time.

Appliqué

The numbers on the master pattern indicate the sewing sequence. Follow the sewing sequence and appliqué. For in-depth coverage of this subject, see Appliqué (pages 32–47), which will give you step-by-step instructions and helpful advice to complete your appliqué project.

TRAPUNTO

I added some trapunto to this quilt. The trapunto must be done before you layer your quilt. Trace the feather design for the trapunto onto the right side of the quilt top with a water-soluble marker. Follow the instructions in Trapunto (page 56) to complete the trapunto.

QUILT ASSEMBLY

1. Trim the center square to 36½″ × 36½″.

2. Sew each inner border strip to an outer border strip, matching the centers.

3. Sew the borders to the center square and miter the corners.

FINISHING

Layer, quilt as desired, and finish by binding the quilt.

Pattern for Trapunto Feather 2

Pattern for Trapunto Feather 1

Trapunto placement

Pattern for Small Rose 1

Pattern for Small Rose 2

Reverse appliqué

Pattern for Small Rose 3

Pattern for Small Rose 4

Pattern for Bow 1

Pattern for Bow 2

Quilt layout

Stevie's Quilt

Finished quilt: 53½″ × 53½″

Not too long ago, a few of my friends and I, a lovely group called Rita's Club, were sitting together stitching various projects. My daughter Stevie was visiting, and one of my friends asked her how many quilts I had made for her. "None," she replied with a smirk on her face, looking from the corner of her eye to see whether I had heard what she had just said. "But all my quilts are for you girls," I protested. (I have another younger daughter.) As soon as a quilt is done, either one or the other of the girls "bombs" the quilt, meaning she claims it as her own. "Yeah, I know," Stevie answered with a sheepish smile, and, glancing around the room as if looking for approval, she said with a bit of a whining voice, "But none of them has my name on it!" We all laughed, and, armed with a permanent micro pen, I inked her name on the letter the dove is carrying, making it officially Stevie's Quilt. I hope you have a daughter or granddaughter you adore as much as I adore mine and can prove it not only by stitching this beautiful quilt but also by putting her name in ink on it.

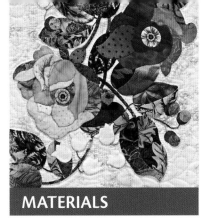

General Instructions: The cutting instructions for background fabrics include a ¼″ seam allowance, which adds up to an additional ½″ for the length and width measurements. Add your favorite seam allowance when you use the templates for the appliqué.

MATERIALS

- **Background:** 1¼ yards white, off-white, or light-colored fabric (A white print on white is harder to appliqué onto.)
- **Fabrics for appliqué:** In this quilt I used some chintz fabric in addition to others from my stash. Choose a variety of tightly woven fabric scraps, from thumb size to fat quarters. If you appliqué a lot as I do, you will find a spot for the last scrap of your favorite fabric, as small as it might be. Maybe the rosebud you will use it for will become your favorite flower in the quilt. For guidance on color and fabric selection, see How to Achieve a Baltimore Look (page 23).

- **Inner border:** ¼ yard red fabric
- **Outer border:** 2 yards
- **Batting:** 61″ × 61″
- **Backing:** 3¾ yards
- **Binding:** ¾ yard

CUTTING

White, Off-White, or Light Color
Background pieces are cut a little larger to allow for tightening during appliqué.
- Cut 1 square 39″ × 39″.

Inner Border (Red)
- Cut 4 strips 1″ × 38½″.

Outer Border
- Cut 4 strips 8″ × 53½″. These measurements might differ depending on the width of the border print you choose. Adjust the measurements as you see fit.

Binding
- Cut binding fabric on the bias into 2″ strips and piece to total 230″ (approximately 6¼ yards).

CONSTRUCTION
Find and Trace Patterns

- Center Rose—pattern pullout page P3
- Stevie's Swag—pattern pullout page P4
- Dove—pattern pullout page P2
- Bird on a Branch—pattern pullout page P3

Note: The gray lines on the patterns indicate places where you might want to add embroidery (page 48) or button flowers (page 59).

For correct placement, find the center of your background fabric and line it up with the center of the rose on the Center Rose master pattern. Trace the rose bouquet with a water-soluble marker onto the background fabric. Follow the quilt layout diagram for correct placement of the other patterns. Trace Stevie's Swag from the master pattern onto the background fabric in the upper left side and the bottom right side of the block. *Note:* For the upper right and bottom left sides, you need to reverse the pattern, as follows.

From your master pattern, make a photocopy of Stevie's Swag.

Place the back of the copy on a lightbox and trace the design onto the upper right and lower left sides of the background fabric.

Trace the Dove and Bird on Branch from the master pattern onto the background fabric. I mark each pattern one at a time, not all at once, as the water-soluble marker may fade over time.

Dove

Bird on branch

Appliqué

The numbers on the master pattern reflect the sewing sequence. Follow the sewing sequence and appliqué. For in-depth coverage of this subject, see Appliqué (pages 32–47), which will give you step-by-step instructions and helpful advice to complete your appliqué project.

QUILT ASSEMBLY

1. Trim the center square to 37½" × 37½".

2. Sew each inner border strip to an outer border strip, matching the centers.

3. Sew the borders to the center square and miter the corners.

FINISHING

Layer, quilt as desired, and finish by binding the quilt.

Quilt layout

RUBY SLIPPER

Ruby Slipper

Finished quilt: 37½″ × 37½″

Whether it is Dorothy in *The Wizard of Oz*, wearing ruby slippers that will bring her back home if she clicks her heels three times, or Karen in Hans Christian Andersen's fairy tale, wearing the red shoes that won't stop dancing, red shoes are magical. Use this Baltimore Album block—a ruby slipper adorned with roses, adding beauty to the magic of the red shoe—for your next Baltimore Album quilt or frame the block with a beautiful border print for a small wallhanging or pillow. I made this little "quilty" for my daughter Stevie, who captured the magic of the red shoes in one of her first photography projects in college. Now that she has made her dream come true, I wonder if the magic of the red shoes had something to do with it. I happen to think so.

General Instructions: The cutting instructions for background fabrics include a ¼" seam allowance, which adds up to an additional ½" for the length and width measurements. Add your favorite seam allowance when you use the templates for the appliqué.

MATERIALS

- **Background:** ¾ yard white, off-white, or light-colored fabric (A white print on white is harder to appliqué onto.)
- **Fabrics for appliqué:** Choose a variety of tightly woven fabric scraps, from thumb size to fat quarters. If you appliqué a lot as I do, you will find a spot for the last scrap of your favorite fabric, as small as it might be. Maybe the rosebud you will use it for will become your favorite flower in the quilt. For guidance on color and fabric selection, see How to Achieve a Baltimore Look (page 23).

- **Inner border:** ¼ yard yellow fabric
- **Outer border:** 1¼ yards
- **Batting:** 45" × 45"
- **Backing:** 2½ yards
- **Binding:** ⅝ yard

CUTTING

White, Off-White, or Light Color
Background pieces are cut a little larger to allow for tightening during appliqué.
- Cut 1 square 20" × 20".

Inner Border (Yellow)
- Cut 4 strips 1" × 19½".

Outer Border
- Cut 4 strips 9½" × 38½". These measurements might differ depending on the width of the border print you choose. Adjust the measurements as you see fit.

Binding
- Cut binding fabric on the bias into 2" strips and piece to total 166" (approximately 4¾ yards).

Enlarge the corner roses as indicated.

CONSTRUCTION

Find and Trace Patterns

- Ruby Slipper Center—page 87
- Corner Flowers—page 88
  Note: Pattern is shown at 75%. Photocopy at 125% to create the full-size pattern.
- The gray lines on the patterns indicate places where you might want to add embroidery (page 48) or button flowers (page 59).

For correct placement, find the center of your background fabric and line it up with the center of the ruby slipper. Trace the pattern with a water-soluble marker onto the background fabric. Following the layout diagram, trace the corner roses onto the left corner and bottom right corner of the background fabric. *Note:* For the upper right and bottom left corners, you need to reverse the pattern, as follows.

Turn the pattern over to the left side.

Place the pattern on a lightbox and trace the pattern onto the background fabric.

Appliqué

The numbers on the pattern reflect the sewing sequence. Follow the sewing sequence and appliqué. For in-depth coverage of this subject, see Appliqué (pages 32–47), which will give you step-by-step instructions and helpful advice to complete your appliqué project.

QUILT ASSEMBLY

1. Trim the center square to 18½″ × 18½″.

2. Sew each inner border strip to an outer border strip, matching the centers.

3. Sew the borders to the center square and miter the corners.

FINISHING

Layer, quilt as desired, and finish by binding the quilt.

Quilt layout

Pattern for Ruby Slipper
Center

Pattern for Corner Flowers—pattern at 75%

Little Basket

Finished quilt: 40½″ × 40½″

My daughter Jessie was visiting when I was working on this Baltimore Album block. "Oh, Mom, is that for me? Can I have it? I love it," she said with a big smile as she was eyeing the block. "Just put some butterflies on it, here and here," she suggested, pointing to a couple of areas on the block. "Then it's perfect!" I think she fell in love immediately with the blue roses. I had seen blue roses in some Baltimore Album blocks. Blue is not a color you think of when you think of roses, but I liked the look and decided to try it. I loved the result and apparently so did my daughter. All my life I have had a bit of a hard time saying no to my children, but this was an easy yes. Now, with her "quilty" in her suitcase, she will carry a bit of home with her wherever she goes.

MATERIALS

General Instructions: The cutting instructions for background fabrics include a ¼" seam allowance, which adds up to an additional ½" for the length and width measurements. Add your favorite seam allowance when you use the templates for the appliqué.

- **Background:** ¾ yard white, off-white, or light-colored fabric (A white print on white is harder to appliqué onto.)
- **Fabrics for appliqué:** Choose a variety of tightly woven fabric scraps, from thumb size to fat quarters. If you appliqué a lot as I do, you will find a spot for the last scrap of your favorite fabric, as small as it might be. Maybe the rosebud you will use it for will become your favorite flower in the quilt. For guidance on color and fabric selection, see How to Achieve a Baltimore Look (page 23).

- **Inner border:** ¼ yard red fabric
- **Middle border:** ½ yard
- **Outer border:** 1 yard
- **Batting:** 48" × 48"
- **Backing:** 1¼ yards
- **Binding:** ¾ yard

CUTTING

White, Off-White, or Light Color
Background pieces are cut a little larger to allow for tightening during appliqué.
- Cut 1 square 20" × 20".

Inner Border (Red)
- Cut 4 strips 1" × 19½".

Middle Border
- Cut 4 strips 3" × 24½".

Outer Border
- Cut 4 strips 8½" × 40½". These measurements might differ depending on the width of the border print you choose. Adjust the measurements as you see fit.

Binding
- Cut binding fabric on the bias into 2" strips and piece to total 178" (approximately 5 yards).

CONSTRUCTION
Find and Trace Patterns

- Little Basket Center—page 92 (*Note:* The pattern is shown at 75%. Photocopy at 125% to create the full-size pattern.)
- Little Corner Flowers—page 94
- Butterfly—page 94

Note: The gray lines on the patterns indicate places where you might want to add embroidery (page 48) or button flowers (page 59).

For correct placement, find the center of your background fabric and line it up with the center of the basket pattern. Trace the basket pattern with a water-soluble marker onto the background fabric. Following the layout diagram, trace the corner roses onto the upper left and bottom right sides of the background fabric. *Note:* For the upper right and lower left sides of the appliqué design, you need to reverse the pattern, as follows.

Turn the pattern over to the left side.

Place the pattern on a lightbox and trace the pattern onto the background fabric.

Appliqué

The numbers on the pattern reflect the sewing sequence. Follow the sewing sequence and appliqué. For in-depth coverage of this subject, see Appliqué (pages 32–47), which will give you step-by-step instructions and helpful advice to complete your appliqué project.

QUILT ASSEMBLY

1. Trim the center square to 18½" × 18½".

2. Sew each inner border strip to an outer border strip, matching the centers.

3. Sew the borders to the center square and miter the corners.

FINISHING

Layer, quilt as desired, and finish by binding the quilt.

Quilt layout

Pattern for Little Basket
Center—pattern at 75%

Basket detail in
Little Basket

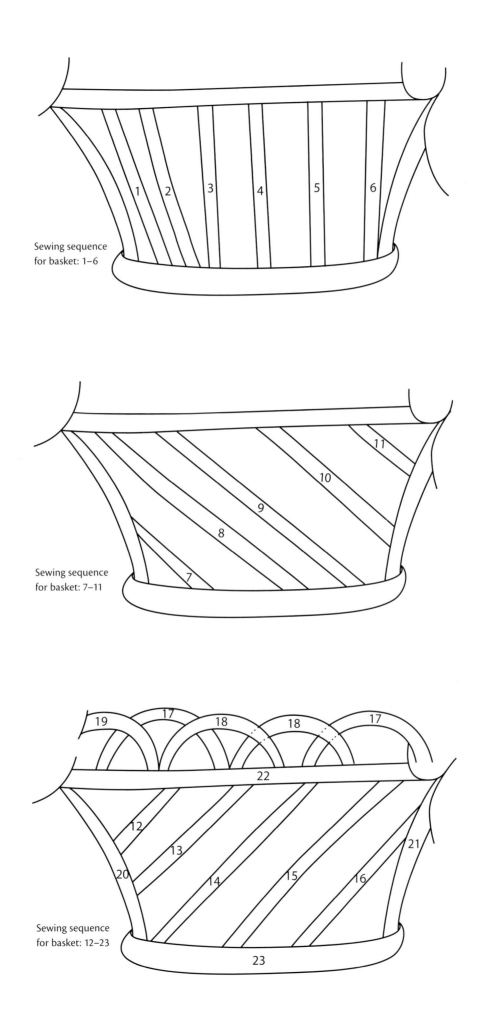

Sewing sequence
for basket: 1–6

Sewing sequence
for basket: 7–11

Sewing sequence
for basket: 12–23

Inked

Inked

Pattern for Butterfly

Pattern for Little
Corner Flowers

About the Author

Photo by Stevie Verroca

Rita Verroca is an award-winning quilter whose quilts have been exhibited in the United States, Europe, Canada, and Japan. Her quilts have been featured on magazine covers and in calendars and quilt books. She has won many awards in international competitions and shows. Rita is a passionate teacher of the fine arts of needle-turn appliqué, hand piecing, and hand quilting. Entirely self-taught, she draws upon two dozen years of sewing experience. She has developed great skills, and she shares her knowledge with her students with contagious enthusiasm. In her quilts, she combines old heritage quilt patterns with delightful new arrangements. Her choice of colors is artful, and the beautiful images are arranged to give the overall design a stimulating and harmonious balance.

Great Titles *from* C&T PUBLISHING & stashBOOKS®

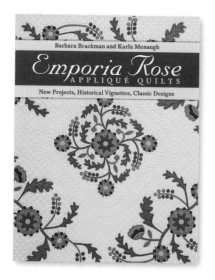

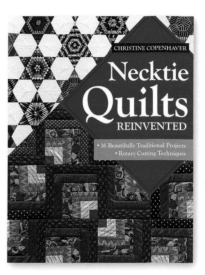

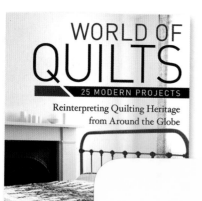

Av   300-284-1114

For a list of other fine
to view our catalog or

C&T PUBLISHIN
P.O. Box 1456
Lafayette, CA 94549
800-284-1114

Tips and techniques c

plies:

ATCH

e.
4549
177 | Email: CottonPa@aol.com
-283-7883 | Website: quiltusa.com

own may not be currently available, as fabric
keep most fabrics in print for only a short time.